# XTREME FISH

# Piranha

## BY S.L. HAMILTON

A&D Xtreme
An imprint of Abdo Publishing | www.abdopublishing.com

# Visit us at
# www.abdopublishing.com

Published by Abdo Publishing Company, a division of ABDO, PO Box 398166, Minneapolis, Minnesota 55439. Copyright ©2015 by Abdo Consulting Group, Inc. International copyrights reserved in all countries. No part of this book may be reproduced in any form without written permission from the publisher. A&D Xtreme™ is a trademark and logo of Abdo Publishing Company.

Printed in the United States of America, North Mankato, Minnesota.
032014
092014

 PRINTED ON RECYCLED PAPER

Editor: John Hamilton
Graphic Design: Sue Hamilton
Cover Design: Sue Hamilton
Cover Photo: Getty Images
Interior Photos: Alamy-pg 8 (bottom); AP-pg 27; Corbis-pgs 13 (bottom), 25 & 28-29; Dreamstime-pg 8 (top); Getty-pgs 4-5, 9, 12, 14-15, 16-17, 18-19, 22 (inset), 24 & 26; National Geographic-pgs 20-21; RavenFire Media-pgs 7 & 15 (inset); Science Source-pgs 10-11 & 22-23; Thinkstock-pgs 1, 2-3, 6, 13 (top), 30-31 & 32.

Websites
To learn more about Xtreme Fish, visit booklinks.abdopublishing.com. These links are routinely monitored and updated to provide the most current information available.

Library of Congress Control Number: 2014932243

Cataloging-in-Publication Data

Hamilton, S. L.
 Piranha / S. L. Hamilton.
  p. cm. -- (Xtreme fish)
Includes index.
ISBN 978-1-62403-450-3
1. Piranhas--Juvenile literature.   2. Marine animals--Juvenile literature.   3. Predatory animals--Juvenile literature.   I. Title.
597/.48--dc23

2014932243

# Contents

Piranha . . . . . . . . . . . . . . . . . . . . . . . . . . . .4

Species & Location . . . . . . . . . . . . . . . . . . . .6

Size . . . . . . . . . . . . . . . . . . . . . . . . . . . . . .8

Shape . . . . . . . . . . . . . . . . . . . . . . . . . . . .10

Shoal Fish . . . . . . . . . . . . . . . . . . . . . . . . .12

Eyesight . . . . . . . . . . . . . . . . . . . . . . . . . . .14

Hearing . . . . . . . . . . . . . . . . . . . . . . . . . . .16

Sense of Smell . . . . . . . . . . . . . . . . . . . . . .18

Lateral Line . . . . . . . . . . . . . . . . . . . . . . . .20

Teeth & Jaws . . . . . . . . . . . . . . . . . . . . . . .22

What Piranha Eat . . . . . . . . . . . . . . . . . . . .24

Attacks on Humans . . . . . . . . . . . . . . . . . .26

Fishing For Piranha . . . . . . . . . . . . . . . . . .28

Glossary . . . . . . . . . . . . . . . . . . . . . . . . . .30

Index . . . . . . . . . . . . . . . . . . . . . . . . . . . . .32

# Piranha

Piranha are freshwater fish known for their fierce feeding skills. Their mouths are filled with sharp teeth designed to rip chunks out of prey. From tooth to tail, piranha have developed amazing abilities that allow them to survive and thrive in the rivers of South America.

**XTREME FACT –** *Native to South America, the word* piranha *comes from the native Tupi-Guarani language meaning "toothed fish."*

# Species & Location

There are about 30 to 60 species of "true piranha" in South America. True piranha are defined as carnivores, or meat eaters, with razor-sharp teeth. Although new species continue to be discovered, piranha have existed for about 15 million years.

*A piranha fossil.*

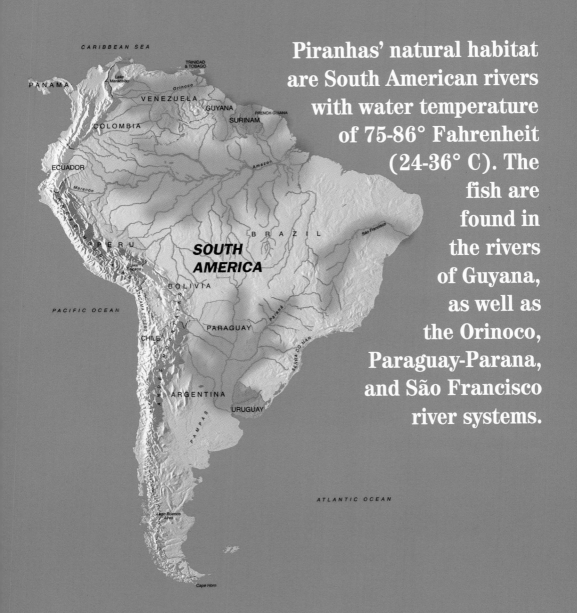

Piranhas' natural habitat are South American rivers with water temperature of 75-86° Fahrenheit (24-36° C). The fish are found in the rivers of Guyana, as well as the Orinoco, Paraguay-Parana, and São Francisco river systems.

XTREME FACT – Piranha are illegal to own as pets in parts of the United States. It is feared that owners will release them into local lakes and streams. They have been found in lakes in Texas, Wisconsin, Michigan, and Missouri.

# Size

Piranha are not big fish. Red-bellied piranha are about 5.5 to 10.25 inches (14-26 cm) long. Adult fish weigh from 3.5 to 7 pounds (1.6-3.2 kg). Black piranha grow to 16 inches (41 cm). The San Francisco piranha is one of the biggest species. It reaches a length of 20 inches (51 cm).

*San Francisco piranha are also known as man-eating piranha.*

Black piranha are gray in color. They are also called redeye piranha.

XTREME FACT–
Piranha are also called "caribe" by the natives of Venezuela, South America.

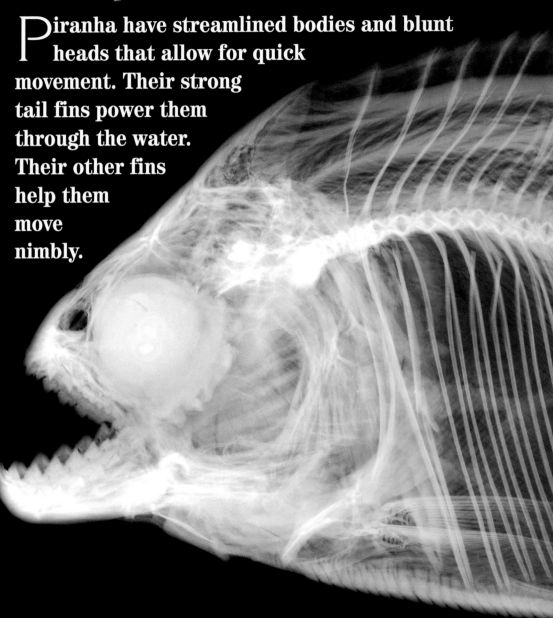

# Shape

Piranha have streamlined bodies and blunt heads that allow for quick movement. Their strong tail fins power them through the water. Their other fins help them move nimbly.

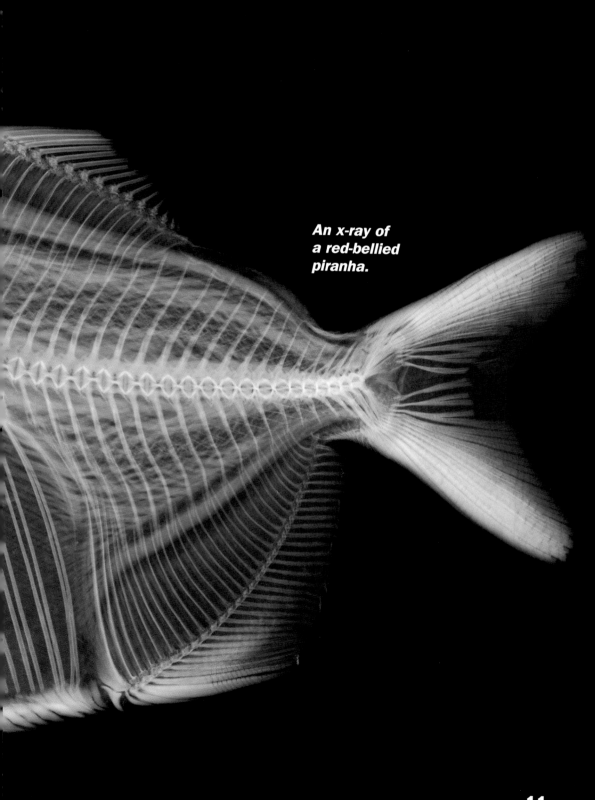

An x-ray of
a red-bellied
piranha.

# Shoal Fish

Since piranha are not big fish, their strength lies in living in a pack, or "shoal." In groups of 20 to 100, piranha can attack their prey in a mass of swift, churning violence. The surface of the water appears to boil during a piranha attack.

A piranha feeding frenzy viewed from above the water.

Piranha eating fish in an aquarium.

*A Brazilian jabiru stork eats a piranha.*

As shoal fish, piranha have safety in numbers from predators who eat them. Even so, many piranha are food for humans, as well as birds such as storks, herons, cormorants, and fish eagles. Piranha are also eaten by freshwater dolphins, catfish, turtles, and caimans. Large piranha eat small piranha.

*A caiman eats a piranha.*

# Eyesight

Piranhas have well-developed senses that help them survive and thrive. Piranha eyes are quite large in relation to their bodies. They see best when there is daylight, but they can see at night also. Scientists believe that piranha can see at least 20 different colors.

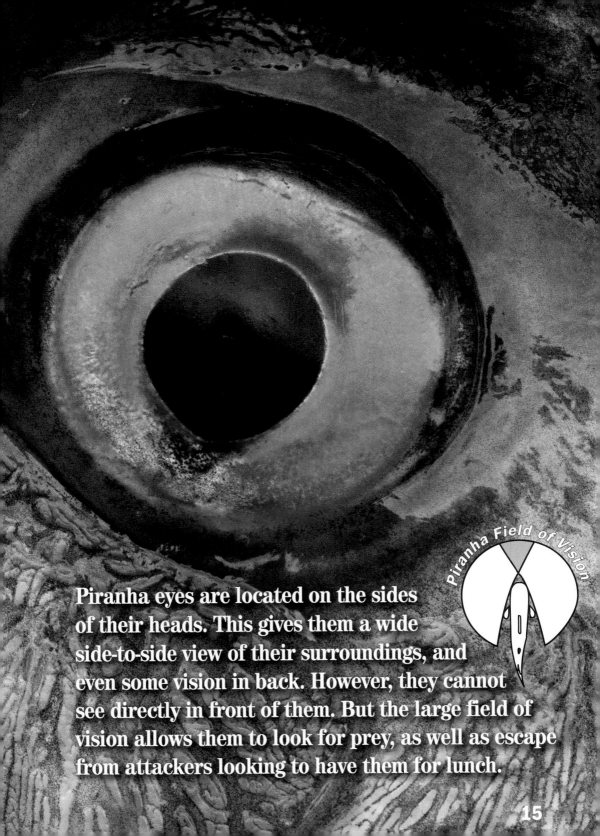

Piranha eyes are located on the sides of their heads. This gives them a wide side-to-side view of their surroundings, and even some vision in back. However, they cannot see directly in front of them. But the large field of vision allows them to look for prey, as well as escape from attackers looking to have them for lunch.

Piranha Field of Vision

# Hearing

Piranha have excellent hearing. They do not have ears like humans. Their hearing organs are located inside their skulls. They listen for splashes indicating that something edible is in trouble. A splash is like a dinner bell to a piranha.

**XTREME FACT**– Piranha use their air bladder to make barking and croaking sounds. The barks are sounded when the fish are facing off against each other. The croaks occur when they bite one another.

# Sense of Smell

A piranha has an excellent sense of smell. Its nostrils are located just behind its mouth. Water enters the nostrils and slides across a highly sensitive olfactory membrane. This membrane sends signals to the brain, giving the piranha detailed information about its surroundings and its prey.

*XTREME FACT – Piranha can smell blood in the water even from a long distance. This ability helps them find food quickly.*

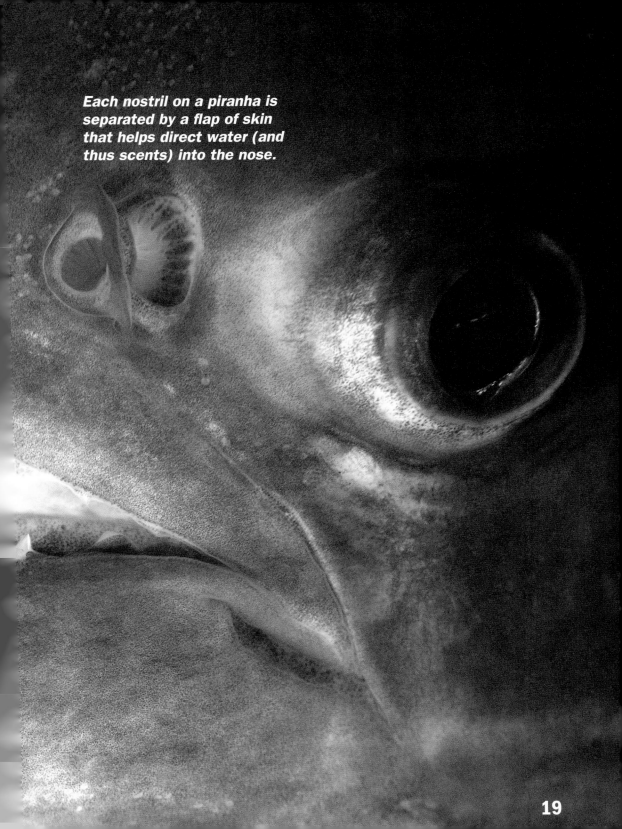

Each nostril on a piranha is separated by a flap of skin that helps direct water (and thus scents) into the nose.

# Lateral Line

Piranhas have a body part, called a lateral line, that helps them sense what's around them. It runs from head to tail along its sides. This organ allows them to sense objects around them in murky water. It helps them avoid rocks and other obstacles.

Lateral Line

The lateral line helps piranha feel movement in the water. They know members of their pack by the way they swim. The lateral line also signals piranha when prey are struggling in the water.

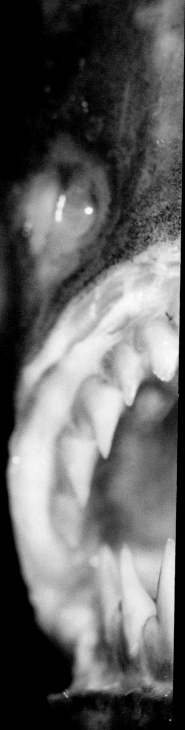

# Teeth & Jaws

True piranha are equipped with sharp teeth and one of the strongest jaws of any living fish. The bigger front teeth are designed for snapping off chunks of meat from prey. The triangular top and bottom teeth lock together when the mouth closes.

*XTREME FACT – Piranha teeth have been used by natives of South America as a type of scissors.*

# What Piranha Eat

Piranha are scavengers, attacking and eating fish, birds, and mammals that are hurt and splashing in the water.

*A man stands over a cow carcass stripped clean by piranha.*

Piranha are sneak attackers. They lurk near a fish, seemingly not paying attention. When the fish isn't watching, a piranha will race up to the unsuspecting victim from behind and take a bite out of its fins or body.

A young red-bellied piranha has bites out of its tail from other piranha.

XTREME QUOTE – "The rabid, furious snaps drive the teeth through flesh and bone."
–President Theodore Roosevelt, writing about piranha in his 1914 book Through the Brazilian Wilderness

# Attacks on Humans

**H**umans are not a piranha's first meal choice, but these fish are not afraid to bite off pieces of meat from creatures far larger than themselves. South American natives often swim safely in piranha-infested waters. Piranha need to be excited by noise or blood before they go into a feeding frenzy.

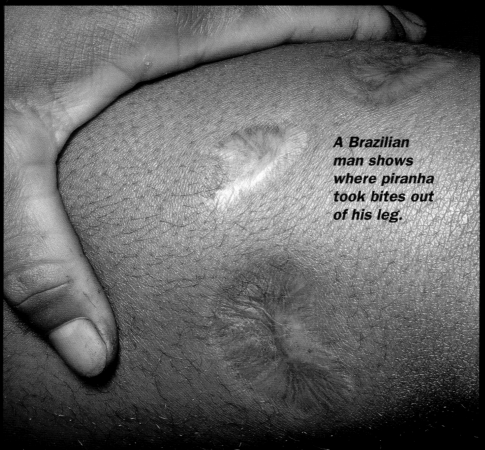

*A Brazilian man shows where piranha took bites out of his leg.*

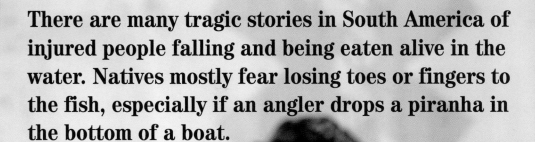

There are many tragic stories in South America of injured people falling and being eaten alive in the water. Natives mostly fear losing toes or fingers to the fish, especially if an angler drops a piranha in the bottom of a boat.

*A man is treated after he was bit by a piranha while wading in Argentina's Parana River.*

> **XTREME FACT** – Piranha teeth are so sharp, humans often cannot feel when the fish take their first bites out of a toe or leg.

# Fishing for Piranha

Piranha are caught by pole and by net. Fishermen attract piranha by slapping the top of the water with their poles or hands. Unlike other fish that are often scared off by sounds, the noise brings in piranha. The trick for some anglers is to get the hooked fish out of the water before other piranha eat it.

**XTREME FACT –** Piranha teeth and jaws are so strong, they are known to bite through fishhooks.

A cowboy from the Pantanal wetlands in southern Brazil holds up his piranha catch.

# Glossary

## AIR BLADDER
A sac inside the body of a fish that holds air. It is also known as a gas bladder or swim bladder. It helps a fish adjust to different water depths. In a piranha, the air bladder also allows the fish to make certain barking and croaking noises.

## CAIMAN
A reptile that looks similar to an alligator. It is found in South American rivers and is known to eat piranha.

## CARNIVORE
A creature that eats meat.

## FEEDING FRENZY
A group attack on prey by a large number of fish. Piranha and sharks are known to go into feeding frenzies.

## FRESHWATER
Water sources with little amounts of salt in them, such as lakes and rivers. Saltwater, such as water in oceans and

### LATERAL LINE
A visible line that runs along
the sides of fish. The lateral line
helps fish detect movement in the
water. The sensing organ helps fish to find prey
and helps them avoid becoming prey.

### OLFACTORY MEMBRANE
Olfactory refers to a sense of smell. The olfactory
membrane refers to a thin layer of tissue that allows
fish to detect smells, such as blood, in the water.

### SCAVENGERS
Creatures that eat what they
can find, including dead and
dying prey.

### SHOAL FISH
Fish that live in a pack for group feeding and protection
from predators. Piranha live in packs of 20-100.

### STREAMLINED
The shape of a creature or object that reduces the drag,
or resistance, of air or water flowing across its surface.
This increases speed and ease of movement. Fish, such
as piranha, have a streamlined shape that allows them
to swim faster because they don't have to push as hard to

# Index

**A**
air bladder  16
Argentina  27

**B**
black piranha  8, 9
Brazil  29

**C**
caiman  13
caribe  9
carnivores  6

**F**
feeding frenzy  12, 26

**G**
Guyana  7

**J**
jabiru stork  13

**L**
lateral line  20, 21

**M**
man-eating piranha  8
Michigan  7
Missouri  7

**O**
olfactory membrane  18
Orinoco River  7

**P**
Pantanal wetlands  29
Paraguay-Parana River
    7, 27

**R**
red-bellied piranha  8,
    11, 25
redeye piranha  9
Roosevelt, Theodore  25

**S**
San Francisco piranha  8
São Francisco River  7
scavengers  24
shoal  12, 13
South America  4, 5, 6,
    9, 22, 27

**T**
Texas  7
*Through the Brazilian
    Wilderness*  25
true piranha  6, 22
Tupi-Guarani  5

**U**
United States  7

**V**
Venezuela  9

**W**
Wisconsin  7